Now
what,
Lord?

From the Best-Selling Series

young **readers**

More than one million sold!

Now what, Lord?

Bible devotions and activities for girls

Barbara Owen

Augsburg

MINNEAPOLIS

NOW WHAT, LORD?
Bible Devotions and Activities for Girls

Scripture quotations unless otherwise noted are from the Holy Bible: New International Version. Copyright 1978 by the New York International Bible Society. Used by permission of Zondervan Bible Publishers.

Scripture quotations identified as TEV are from Today's English Version of the Bible, copyright 1976 American Bible Society, and are used by permission.

Photos courtesy of Images © 1995 PhotoDisc, Inc., cover; Jean-Claude Lejeune, pp. 12, 40; David Hiebert, p. 16; Roger W. Neal, p. 65; Gallery of Images—Burkey photo, p. 70; Hildegard Adler, p. 108.

Cover design by Craig P. Claeys

Library of Congress Cataloging-in-Publication Data

Webb, Barbara Owen
  Now What, Lord?

  Summary: Directed towards girls, presents Bible and contemporary stories, activities, suggested readings, and prayers relating to siblings, gossip, death, friendship, love, and other topics.
  1. Girls—Prayer books and devotions—English.
  [1. Prayer books and devotions. 2. Christian life.
  3. Conduct of life] I. Title.
  BV4860.W43   1985   242'833   85-22884
  ISBN 0-8066-2182-6

The paper used in this publication meets the minimum requirements of American National Standard for Information Sciences—Permanence of Paper for Printed Library Materials, ANSI Z329.48-1984.   ∞

Manufactured in the U.S.A.   AF 9-2182

00 99 98 97 96   10 11 12 13 14 15 16 17 18

For Aunt Marion

Contents

About This Book

As you get into the last years of grade school, your ideas about yourself and life seem to grow and change. So does your relationship with God. You want to know him better, understand more about him and his Word. You have questions you wish he'd answer. When life seems to be going smoothly, suddenly everything goes topsy-turvey. "Now what, Lord?" you wonder in your prayers.

God's people through the ages have had this question for him. Noah faithfully built the ark and boarded it when the rain began. During that long time, cooped up with all those animals, watching the pouring rain, coping with smells and seasickness, he must have asked often, "Now what, Lord?"

Sarah faithfully went along with her husband Abraham to the new land God was giving them. She got there and found they would have to live in tents, sometimes among hostile people. A baby was promised, but Sarah kept getting older and older with no child. "Now what, Lord?" she must have wondered.

The apostle Paul had a special calling from Jesus to preach the good news of salvation. But often he ended up in jail. "Now what, Lord?" he must have prayed.

In the case of each of these faithful people, God used the unexpected situation. Land did appear for Noah and he was given a special sign—the rainbow. At last Sarah become a mother to Isaac, beginning a mighty nation. Paul used his time in prison to write many letters that are now a part of the Bible.

God is working in your life too. Sometimes you won't see how until you look back months later. But when you're puzzled and pray, "Now what, Lord?" guidance will come, sometimes in surprising ways. The devotions in this book show God working in the lives of Bible people and in the lives of girls your age. May you find a surer trust in him, especially at those times when *you* might ask, "Now what, Lord?"

1 What Are You Going to Be When You Grow Up?

You, Lord, are all I have, and you gave me all I need; my future is in your hands.

Psalm 16:5

Young David looked out at the mighty Goliath. Who was to fight this huge Philistine? The soldiers shook their heads. David, the shepherd boy, tested the cords of his slingshot. The Lord had always supplied all David's needs when he defended the sheep against wild animals. Wouldn't the Lord take care of him now if he fought Goliath, the enemy of God's people?

"I'll fight," David volunteered, putting his whole future in the Lord's hands.

David not only beat Goliath, he went on to be king. He became one of the most beloved people of the Old Testament because of his faith during all sorts of difficult times.

Today's Bible verse is from a psalm that expresses the kind of faith David had in God, even as a young person.

David hadn't planned to be king. But he put his trust in God and used the abilities God had given him. The Lord guided David and made him a blessing to people in his day and for others through the years. We too can trust our futures to God, especially since we know the greatest proof of his love for us—Jesus Christ.

Janet wondered about her future as she sat on the school bus. "Why do grown-ups always want to know what you're going to be when you grow up?" she asked her friend Anne. "I mean, who *knows*?"

"Not me," laughed Anne. "I don't even know whether to take typing or music next year in junior high. Who's been asking?"

Janet braced herself as the bus creaked to a stop. "My aunt; she's visiting from Seattle. I should have asked *her* when *she* knew what she was going to be. Maybe I will."

At home, Janet found her aunt in the kitchen making a cup of tea. Pouring a glass of milk and

13

taking two Oreos, Janet began. "Aunt Sue, when did you know that you wanted to be a pediatric nurse?"

"Always, I guess," Aunt Sue answered. "At least since fifth grade when I realized how much I liked baby-sitting."

"Oh." Janet groaned inside. How could anyone be so sure in fifth grade?

"But that hardly ever happens," her aunt continued. "Most of my friends didn't know until after high school or even later."

"Really?" Janet felt a relieved surprise. "That's like me and my friend Anne. We don't even know what classes to take in junior high. I'm just going to take what sounds interesting and see where it leads."

"Good." Aunt Sue stirred her tea thoughtfully. "There's a verse in Proverbs that says, 'Commit your work to the Lord, and your plans will be established.' You can pray for guidance, then go ahead and follow your interests, trusting that God is guiding you. After all, God gave you your abilities and interests."

"And if I get off course, God will steer me back, right?" Janet licked the icing out of the middle of an Oreo.

"Right; that's trust."

Janet felt better as she went to do her homework. The answer to the question was, "I don't know yet, but God does and that's enough."

14

Action Idea: List on a piece of paper three things you like to do. Then list three things you do well. Does something appear on both lists? Pray that God will show you how to use it for others. You can be a blessing as David was, and God may use these interests for your future.

Bible Reading Extra: Psalm 16:5-11

Prayer: *Dear Jesus, you have taken care of me always. You are with me now. I trust you with my future. Guide me in using the interests and abilities that are gifts from you. Amen.*

2 Even Baseball?

Do to others as you would have them do to you.
Luke 6:31

You have probably heard this verse before. It has been called the golden rule, perhaps because life would be so pleasant if everyone did this. Anyone reading the verse would say, "Yes, that sounds like a very good idea." But what happens? We get angry or selfish or forgetful. Then we aren't treating others the way we would like to be treated. We are yelling, not sharing, forgetting to be a friend.

At such times we remember the One who spoke the golden rule—Jesus. He is the only one who could say this because he behaved this way on earth. No one touched lepers—Jesus healed them. No decent

17

person had a tax collector for a friend—Jesus made one a disciple. No one thought about hungry crowds—Jesus fed them. No men spoke to women in public—Jesus shared the good news. No one wanted to be with sinners—Jesus took everyone's sin on himself.

Jesus really lived this golden rule. Now he encourages us to do so in following his example. He gives us his Holy Spirit to help. And when we fail, he is the one who will forgive us. What a friend we have in Jesus! He can help us to be friends to others.

In center field Janet raced to her left, keeping her eyes on the high fly ball. She stretched; the ball dropped hard into her mitt, stinging her hand for a moment.

"Way to go, Janet!" screamed Anne who'd been pitching. The final out clinched the game for Mrs. Berg's room. The whole class cheered. Even the new girl who used a wheelchair was there.

"Let's get a drink," Janet said to Anne, pulling her toward the outdoor drinking fountain. "Sure wish you could go to the Oriole game Saturday. Can't you get out of baby-sitting?"

"I wish I could." Anne nodded toward the girl in the wheelchair. "Why don't you ask Beth? She always watches the school games."

"But I hardly know her," Janet protested. The girls walked in silence toward the school. Finally Janet said, "I guess if *I* was new at school, I'd want to see a pro game."

Later she found Beth going toward the library. "I've got an extra ticket for the Oriole game Saturday," Janet mumbled. "If you'd like to go with me and my family, we could—" How in the world would they get Beth into the family car? Rats! Why had Anne got her into this?

But it was too late. Beth grinned. "Oh, neat! I've only seen one other big league game and that was back in second grade." As if seeing Janet's concern, she continued. "I have a special board that helps me slide right from the wheelchair onto a car seat. I won't be any trouble. I'll have to miss bowling, but that's OK."

"Bowling?" Janet couldn't help staring at Beth's fragile legs.

"In a wheelchair league," Beth explained. "We do it every Saturday. Hey, maybe you could come sometime!"

Janet felt good inside. Her tense muscles relaxed and she reached a hand out to rest on the arm of her new friend. "Yeah, that would be neat. Now let me write down where you live."

Action Idea: By sharing her interest in baseball, Janet was following the golden rule. Write down the name of someone with whom you might share one of your own special interests. Can you make plans to do the sharing?

Bible Reading Extra: John 15:11-17

Prayer: *Dear Jesus, thank you for freeing me from my sins. I can stop looking at myself. I can look around at others and share with them all that you have given me. Help me to do this. Amen.*

3   But What Will I Say?

What joy it is to find just the right word for the right occasion!

Proverbs 15:23 TEV

Who wouldn't agree with today's scripture verse? The right word at the right time can bring joy, happiness, friendship, the good news of God's love. The wrong word can mean misunderstanding, anger, even war.

God's people have often asked him for the right word at crucial times. When God instructed Moses to bring his people out of Egypt, Moses worried about what he would say. He didn't know how to talk to the Israelites or to the king of Egypt. But again and again God helped Moses to speak. And at last God's people were freed from slavery in Egypt.

Jesus knew his disciples wouldn't know how to tell other people about the good news of salvation. "Don't worry. I'll send my Holy Spirit to help you," he told them.

And he did. The first time Peter preached after the Holy Spirit came, 3000 people were converted! The book of Acts shows how God's friends had the right words for others, sometimes in groups, sometimes when one person spoke to another. Philip rode along in a carriage with an official from Ethiopia. The official asked questions about the Bible. Philip had the right words to answer. The man became a Christian.

Of course not everyone was converted. But the disciples used everyday opportunities to talk about their Savior. They enjoyed talking about Jesus, knowing he would give them the right words.

Janet and Beth cheered for the Orioles at the ball game. They saw a TV camera focused on the players. Sometimes it scanned the crowd. Janet and Beth grinned and waved.

The Orioles finally won, 5-4. "Wonder if girls will ever play on major league teams," Janet said riding home after the game. She and Beth sat in the back seat. "I can see myself now—number 5."

Beth giggled. "Maybe you could see yourself tomorrow on TV. My dad said he'd record the game on videotape. Want to come over tomorrow morning and watch?"

Janet frowned. "Well, not in the morning. We go to church and Sunday school in the morning."

"Oh," Beth said.

"What about coming with me in the morning—to church—and we could watch the video in the afternoon? Would that be OK, dad?"

"Sure," he said. "We'd be glad to pick you up, Beth." Janet saw his eyes glance at her in the rearview mirror.

Beth shrugged. "What do you do in church?"

"Well, we sing and pray and—and worship," Janet tried to explain.

"What do you mean—worship? I don't know anything about church."

"Do you know about Jesus?" Janet asked softly.

Beth shook her head.

Wow, thought Janet. *Where do I begin? What do I say?* "He's kind of my best friend. Praying is talking to him. He's God's Son who came to earth a long time ago so people could see how much God loves them."

Beth blinked and stared at Janet. "You really believe that?"

"Yes, I do," said Janet. She smiled as she felt a great assurance inside. "I really do."

"OK," said Beth, grinning now herself. "I'll come and see what church is all about."

That night, Janet lay in bed thinking about how the Orioles won the game. She thanked God for helping her share her faith with Beth. "Now what, Lord? She's coming to church with me tomorrow. I'll just leave it to you."

Action Idea: Janet first shared her interest in base-ball. Then she found she could share her faith in Jesus. Have you tried sharing Jesus with a friend? If you're shy about talking, try sending a get-well card to a sick friend. In your own words, mention Jesus' love. Say that you are praying for the friend. If your church lists people who are sick or homebound, you could begin there.

Bible Reading Extra: Colossians 4:5-6

Prayer: *Dear Lord, thank you for the people who have said the right words about you to me. Help me to bless others with words. Amen.*

4 What's Your Will, God?

"Then you will know the truth, and the truth will set you free."

John 8:32

As Jesus went about teaching, some of the people listened. To them he said, "If you hold to my teaching, you are really my disciples. Then you will know the truth, and the truth will set you free."

What was this teaching they were to obey? For some of the Jewish people at that time, freedom from sin meant obeying all the rules and regulations of their religion. How could Jesus imply that people who were doing this didn't know the truth, that they were not free?

But the teaching Jesus talked about was trust in himself as God's Son. In other words, if people would trust him, they would be free from God's judgment. They would be God's children, too. Free from the power of sin, they could help others in need.

After the death and resurrection of Jesus many people believed that he really was God's Son. They found the freedom Jesus talked about. They were free to serve God by using their different abilities for the good of others.

Janet sat in a pew next to Beth in her wheel-chair. *Would Beth understand the sermon?* Janet wondered, nervously. After all, Beth had never been to church before. *Would she ask questions Janet couldn't answer later?* Beth had seemed to enjoy singing the hymns and the liturgy, but now the pastor was beginning the sermon. He announced the text.

They asked him, "What can we do in order to do what God wants us to do?"

Jesus answered, "What God wants you to do is to believe in the one he sent."

Janet enjoyed the sermon about faith in Jesus. It seemed like a good one for a new person in church to hear.

After the service, at the fellowship hour, the two girls had juice and donuts. Beth met some of Janet's Sunday school friends.

It wasn't until the girls rode home in the car that Janet learned what Beth was thinking.

"It sounds so simple," Beth said in a low voice, almost as if she were thinking out loud. "Just believe in Jesus as God's Son; then I'm God's child too?"

Janet smiled and nodded.

"I always thought church told you how to behave, that you had to behave that way for God to like you," Beth went on.

"Sometimes we learn about being kind or gentle, but not like a rule," Janet said. "When you know how much God loves you, you just want to be kind like he is."

"And God planned for Jesus to come for a long time before he came? Is that what your pastor said?"

"Right. People called prophets told how a Savior would come so people could be right with God. Jesus came and taught and healed and died and rose again. Then he went back to heaven to rule. Even so, he can be with us right here."

"I think I like that," said Beth. "He does seem like a friend. I'll tell my mom and dad. Maybe they'll want to go to church too."

"Sure," Janet agreed. "But if that doesn't work out, you can keep coming with us."

Action Idea: Do you have a friend you could invite to a worship service, Sunday school, or a youth group activity? Pray about your friends who don't go to church. Maybe some of them have the wrong idea about church as Beth did. Decide on a plan to invite a friend to church.

Bible Reading Extra: John 6:28-29

Prayer: *Dear Jesus, you are my Savior and friend. Help me to do God's will by always trusting you. Then I can be free to be me, the person you created me to be. Help me to tell others about the freedom you give. Amen.*

ANNE

1 I'm Not My Sister!

[Jesus answered] ". . . rejoice that your names are written in heaven."

Luke 10:20

Besides Jesus' 12 close disciples, there were many others who followed Jesus. They believed what he said. Jesus decided it was time to send some out to do missionary work. He sent about 70 people to many towns to tell the good news of sins forgiven, to heal sick people and to cast out demons.

When these people returned, they were very excited. Jesus had given them power to do his work. "You should have seen it," they said. "Even demons obeyed us when we used your name." How pleased they were with their accomplishments!

No doubt Jesus was pleased with their work too,

but he told them that this wasn't the real reason to be glad. The real reason for a disciple to be glad is because the disciple's name is written in heaven. The real reason for joy is not because of something we accomplish with God's power. Our joy should come because we are Christians. Our sins are forgiven. We are free to live as friends and children of God.

Jesus told his disciples this. They needed to stop looking at themselves and what they had accomplished with Jesus' power. They were simply to be thankful that their names were "written in heaven."

Anne felt herself sinking down in her school desk as the teacher handed back the poetry notebooks.

"Nice poems, Anne, but why don't you get Stephanie to help you with notebook covers."

Anne took her book, covered with blue construction paper and pasted with some magazine pictures. *Everytime!* she thought, *Stephanie this, Stephanie that.* She was sick of hearing about her older sister's wonderful accomplishments.

The sister comparison was still bothering her after school. She baby-sat with Jill, her two-month-old half-sister. "By the time you get to school, the teachers will have forgotten Stephanie and me. You can just be you," she told the infant, changing her diaper.

Her step-brother Jack, who was a senior in high school, peeked in the nursery to see the baby. "What's eating you?" he said to Anne.

Anne wondered if Jack would understand. Her mother and Jack's father had just been married a little over a year. Anne still wasn't always comfortable with her new family. But Jack did have an older brother who was away at college.

"Did your teachers ever compare you with your older brother?" she asked tentatively. She tidied the pins and powder and things on the changing table.

Jack cuddled the baby. "Did they ever! I thought I'd be through with that since I'm a senior, but the typing teacher never misses a chance to say what a natural my brother was at typing."

Anne felt a sudden sense of comradeship with Jack.

He went on. "It doesn't bother me much now, but a long time ago I got really mad at a teacher and said, 'Look, I'm not my brother!' But that didn't help. It was my pastor who understood. In classes he never compared me with my brother. One day I told him I appreciated that."

"So, what'd he say?" Anne asked as they started downstairs with baby Jill.

"He said God frees us from sin so each of us can be the unique person God made. We don't have to copy someone else. He showed me some Bible verses that show our happiness isn't because of being like Jesus or like anyone else. Our happiness is because our names are in heaven. Now when a teacher tells me how neat my brother is, I agree, knowing he's himself and I'm myself."

Action Idea: You are a special person for God. He made you with unique talents and abilities. He made others in your family with other talents. But the big rejoicing is because Jesus died for you. Write down some of the talents of others in your family. Write down some of your own. Can you see how all are needed in life? Thank God for the abilities of family members and yourself.

Bible Reading Extra: Psalm 139:1-6, 13-15

Prayer: *Lord Jesus, you died so my name could be written in heaven. How I thank you! I thank you for the members of my family and their abilities. Bless each person in my family in using talents from you. In your name. Amen.*

2 Half-sisters and Step-brothers

[Jesus answered] "Whoever does God's will is my brother and sister and mother."

Mark 3:35

Jesus talked to great crowds of people. He spoke intimately with his 12 disciples. Everything that he did in healing and casting out demons, everything he talked about, was to show that he was the promised Savior sent by God. He wanted very much for people to believe him. Then they would know God by knowing the Son.

So one day, when he was talking, Jesus' mother Mary and his brothers stopped by. The message was sent to Jesus: "Your mother and brothers are here. They'd like to talk with you."

Family relationships were very important and people were known by the family they belonged to. Jesus saw this as a chance to show even more important relationships among people. He answered, "Who are my mother and my brothers?" The people must have thought, *What does he mean? They're right outside.*

After catching their attention with the question, Jesus explained. "Whoever does God's will is my brother and sister and mother." The people looked at each other. They could be as close to Jesus as his very own mother and brothers! Other teachers made themselves seem much greater than those they taught. This Jesus wanted the people to be part of his family. Many of the people must have listened more carefully to this amazing Jesus.

Anne held her baby half-sister, Jill, as she waited with the rest of her family. They were seated in chairs in a room at church, waiting for the photographer to take a family picture. The church was getting pictures of all the members to make a picture directory. It would be like the regular directory with names, phone numbers and addresses. But it would have pictures, too.

Because Anne's mother and father had been divorced and her mother remarried, Anne had a sister, a baby half-sister, and two older step-brothers. Sometimes she thought she needed to explain the different relationships to people. Sometimes she thought it was fun to have different people in her family. But other times she

34

wished her family was still her old family of her father, mother and sister.

Finally the time came for the picture. The photographer took several shots. Two weeks later, Anne's mom decided on the one for the church directory. Two months later the directory was finished.

Anne's Sunday school teacher gave out some of the first copies. "Wow, Joe, I didn't know you had such a *big* family," Anne said to the boy next to her as she paged through the directory.

"Some are step-sisters and step-brothers, and I've got a half-brother too," Joe explained.

"That's like my family!" Anne said, showing their picture.

"The whole directory is really a family album," the Sunday school teacher said. "That's why I wanted you to look at it today. Maybe it will help you understand our Scripture about being Jesus' brothers and sisters."

"Oh," said Anne, "then if we're Jesus' brothers and sisters, Joe's my brother and I'm his sister. We're *all* family."

"Right. Look through the directory and get to know your aunts and uncles and cousins and brothers and sisters. There is going to be a Baptism during the service this morning. Pastor will say, 'This is our new brother in Christ.' Really think of him as part of our big family here."

Action Idea: Anne was a little troubled by the different relationships in her family at home. It helped to learn the bigger importance of being sisters and brothers to Jesus and to other Christians. Next time there's a Baptism at your church, pray for that person as a new family member. Send a friendly note saying you're happy to have the person as a new brother or sister. If a baby is baptized, send the note to the parents. If an older child or adult is baptized, send the note to that person.

Bible Reading Extra: Matthew 12:46-50

Prayer: *Lord Jesus, how wonderful it is to be your sister! You are my Savior and brother, too. Please give me brotherly help so I can help others in our big family. Thank you forever. Amen.*

ANNE

3 Funny or Mean?

. . . be kind and tender-hearted to one another. . . .
Ephesians 4:32 TEV

The letter that St. Paul wrote to the church at Ephesus and the surrounding territory was written from
prison. It's one of several called "The Captivity Letters." In this letter he talks about the church, the
family of God. Then he goes on to say how people
in this family will want to treat each other with love.

Paul wants to give some idea of how that love will
act. He wants to show that it's a caring kind of love.
God became a human being in Jesus. Now people
can show their love for God by loving other human
beings.

Paul gets specific. He says Christians should not
shout insults or be hateful toward each other. People

in God's family should not be bitter or lie to each other. Instead, Paul reminds the people that they can be forgiving of each other because God forgave them. Paul puts it very nicely when he says be "tender-hearted." This is a gentle sort of love that looks for the good things about another person. It is the love that wants the best for the other person. Jesus was "tender-hearted" in loving us and forgiving us by dying for us. If we are his brothers and sisters, then we will want to be tender-hearted toward each other in the family.

Anne hurried to her Sunday school room. Her friend Janet was already there.

"Where's Beth?" Anne asked. She knew their friend in a wheelchair usually came with Janet.

"Her parents are coming to church today. They're bringing her," Janet said excitedly. "I hope they want to keep coming. It would be neat for their family to worship together."

Anne nodded just as the classroom door banged shut. Liz dashed in and plopped in a seat. "Shorty's coming down the hall," she said.

"Shorty? Oh, Liz," giggled one of the students.

"She means Beth," explained one of the boys. "Better open the door so she'll know we're here. She's so short in that wheelchair, she can't see in the window part."

"Shorty," giggled someone else. "That's funny. I never thought of that."

"It's not funny. It's mean," said Anne. She felt

her ears getting red and warm, but she'd heard enough. "There's a difference, you know."

"*Funny* is fun for all," added Janet. "But *mean* can hurt feelings."

Liz looked puzzled. "I wasn't trying to be mean," she said. "These funny ideas come to me all the time and I just say them. Beth's OK by me."

Anne sighed and looked at Liz. "I don't think you really meant to be mean either."

"I'll open the door," Liz said. "Here's Beth now."

Action Idea: Do you know someone like Liz who makes funny remarks so easily? But sometimes they're not funny. We all need to think before we speak. Is what we're saying kind? Does it show that we're *tender-hearted?* If you've had this problem, listen to what you say in the next week. Pray that God will help you listen before you speak.

Bible Reading Extra: Isaiah 55:6-7

Prayer: *O Jesus, you were so very kind and tender-hearted with people when you were here on earth. Help me to forgive others and be kind to them, too. Show me how to be tender-hearted toward _____. Amen.*

1 Daydreams

Be careful how you think; your life is shaped by your thoughts.

Proverbs 4:23 TEV

Sayings from the first part of the book of Proverbs come from ancient writings. The sayings had proven true over many years and were worth writing down.

In Old Testament times one great danger for God's people was forgetting God's goodness. Many Bible stories show how the people started thinking about other gods, forgetting the true God. Their lives became selfish and self-centered.

Some of the prophets wrote about the rich people who thought only about money and how to get more money. These people weren't kind and generous toward the poor. Their constant thoughts about money

41

shaped their lives. Their lives were spent getting money and using it for themselves.

We know that when the Wise Men came to Herod, looking for the baby Jesus, Herod thought only of his own power. He was afraid that Jesus would take this power. His greedy thoughts led to murderous thoughts. Trying to get rid of Jesus, Herod had many infants killed.

But a very old lady named Anna had different thoughts. She was a widow who spent her time praying and thinking about God's promised Messiah. When Jesus' parents brought him as a baby to the Temple, Anna knew in her loving thoughts that God's gift had arrived. She spent the rest of her time telling others the good news.

Laurie had some thinking to do too. She stared at the chalkboard but didn't really see it. In her mind she saw herself going into the pet shop, asking to speak to the manager. "I'm interested in the part-time job you advertised," she'd say. The man would look at her coolly. "You're rather young," he'd say. She would stand a little taller and say, "I'm almost 12 and I've had assorted pets all my life." She smiled—assorted pets—that sounded good.

"Laurie!" Mr. Harvey's sharp call made her jump. "If you've finished the assignment, get an extra-credit book to read. Keep your mind on something worthwhile." He shook his head. "Daydreams."

Laurie shuffled to the back of the room. What was wrong with daydreams, she wondered. How else could a person figure out things that were important?

"Try Wendy Watson's new book," Mr. Harvey said. "She'll be our speaker-of-the-month in November."

Wendy Watson? Coming to John Kennedy Elementary? Laurie had always loved Wendy Watson's dog and horse books. Laurie put aside pet store thoughts and picked up *Stephanie's Silver Stallion* by Wendy Watson.

Three weeks later the author sat in front of the class, talking about her new book. Laurie was the first to raise her hand when the question period came.

"How do you plan what will happen in your stories?"

"I do a lot of staring out the window," Wendy Watson said. "I 'see' and 'hear' stories in daydreams before I put anything on paper. Some people think daydreams are a waste of time. It all depends what you daydream about."

"I've been daydreaming about getting a job at a pet store," Laurie said.

"Oh, is that a possibility?" Wendy Watson seemed really interested.

"A job was advertised. Maybe I'm too young, but I know a lot about animals and I've read all your books."

The woman laughed. "Thank you. My books

won't help you get the job, but if you've had experience with animals, maybe you'll be hired. Your daydreams will probably help you be confident when you apply. Just don't put it off too long."

"I won't," Laurie said aloud, thinking to herself that she was about ready, just like when Wendy Watson was ready to stop daydreaming and start writing. Yes, she was ready to act.

Action Idea: What you think about determines what kind of person you are. Satan knows this and sometimes sends unkind and nasty thoughts your way. But Jesus understands this from his own experience here on earth. He will help you keep your mind on better things so daydreaming can be a creative experience. What sort of daydreams or thoughts have you had in the past couple of days that would fit the description in Philippians 4:8?

Bible Reading Extra: Philippians 4:8

Prayer: *Lord, you have made amazing and wonderful minds for people. We can do so many kinds of thinking. Bless my thoughts, daydreams, and imagination today. Amen.*

2   He Makes Me So Mad!

If you become angry, do not let your anger lead you into sin, and do not stay angry all day.
                                    Ephesians 4:26 TEV

A number of little churches had begun around the area of Ephesus. The apostle Paul, in prison, was concerned that these churches continue to grow and preach the good news about Jesus. He wrote them a letter reminding them that the church is not a little club. It is God's special creation, a kind of family.

As in all families, squabbles could arise. Some people might get very angry. Perhaps some people would stop worshiping together because of anger. Paul wanted to remind the people that they might disagree, they might even get angry. But as brothers and sisters in God's family, Paul encouraged them to settle their differences. Then they wouldn't be tempted to sin against each other by hate or spite or in other mean ways.

Paul knew how crafty the devil is. Once he sees anger, he jumps in and tries to make things worse for people. After awhile things get so bad that it is very hard for people to be friends again. So Paul says, "Look, I know you'll get angry from time to time. But work out your problems with God's help. Don't give the devil a chance."

Laurie pumped up the tires on her bike. This afternoon she would go to the pet shop to see about the job.

Her brother Ted sauntered out of the house, swinging the keys to the car. "You really think that guy's going to hire a kid like you?" he said in a know-it-all voice. "What a dreamer!"

"You don't know everything," Laurie retorted.

"I know nobody's going to hire an eleven-year-old." Ted got behind the wheel of the car, opening the window. "Everybody knows you gotta be sixteen."

"Everybody knows most people get their driver's license on the first try, too. But you flunked so mom still has to ride with—" She stopped short as mom came out of the house.

Mom looked back and forth between the two, seeming to suspect something was going on. But she didn't say anything. She slid in on the passenger side of the car. "Good luck at the interview, honey," she called to Laurie as Ted backed out of the driveway.

I hope he flunks again this time, Laurie thought. *I hope he never gets his driver's license.* "Bad luck on your test, Ted!" she yelled after the car.

That evening at the dinner table there was little conversation. Ted and Laurie glared at each other across their mashed potatoes. *If he hadn't said that stuff, I wouldn't have lost my nerve. Now I'll have to try the interview tomorrow,* Laurie thought. She wondered if Ted parked weird because of what she said to him. *Serves him right.*

After dinner, mom asked Laurie to go for a walk with her. "I heard everything that went on between you and Ted this afternoon. It ended up ruining both your days."

"It was his fault," Laurie said. "Did you hear what he said first?"

"Yes, and he was wrong. But he was only teasing."

Laurie opened her mouth in exasperation but nothing came out.

"Sometimes teasers are best put off by almost agreeing with them instead of getting angry. Suppose you'd said, 'Maybe he'll hire me, maybe he won't. We'll see.' That would have kept the anger away. You might be able to break his teasing habit that way."

"I suppose," Laurie said thoughtfully. She smiled. "We'll see."

Action Idea: Teasing can be one of the biggest causes of anger between family members. Teasing hurts because often there's some truth in the tease as in Laurie's case. But teasing is unkind. Almost agreeing with the teaser is often a way to stop the teasing. Since God accepts you as you are, you don't have to prove yourself to others. You can break the teasing chain with a noncommital "You may be right. We'll see." Is there a teasing chain you'd like to break? Ask God to help.

Bible Reading Extra: James 1:19-20

Prayer: *Dear Jesus, sometimes* _____ *makes me so mad! The teasing hurts my feelings. But you love me just as I am. I don't want anger to lead me into sin. Help me in my relationship with* _____ *because you love us both. Amen.*

3 Sometimes I'm a Worrywart

Do not be anxious about anything, but in everything, by prayer and petition, with thanksgiving, present your requests to God.

Philippians 4:6

The people at the church at Philippi were poor. They suffered various troubles and were persecuted because they believed in Jesus Christ. Yet the Apostle Paul tells them in this letter not to worry. Just pray, he says, thanking God when you pray.

How could Paul tell them not to worry when they were poor and persecuted? Paul could say this from experience. He knew that thankful prayer worked. He wrote from prison. He had suffered many persecutions. But he kept praying, thankfully, because he knew God heard and answered prayer.

The people in Philippi had been part of an answered prayer for Paul. As poor as they were, they had gathered a gift and sent it to Paul to help supply his needs in prison. How thankful Paul was to God and to the Philippians!

So we see that these words were not written by someone basking in the sun, sipping a soda. They were written by someone who would seem to have every reason to worry and to grumble to God. Paul may have said "Now what, Lord?" but with a sure expectation of the Lord's generous care.

Laurie woke up early. This afternoon she would go to the pet store to ask about the job. Nothing would stop her today. Again she rehearsed what she would say, *I wish it were over with*, she thought. She opened her Bible to try to chase away her nervousness.

"Don't worry about anything," she read, " . . . ask God for what you need . . . with a thankful heart."

"Well, God," she prayed, "I am worried, so I'll just tell you about it. I *am* thankful that you care, that you listen. You know how much I'd like that job, working with the animals. I'd really like a way to make some extra money, something besides baby-sitting." She gave a deep sigh, not knowing what else to say. So she said the Lord's Prayer, trying to think hard about each petition. Then she was up and soon off to school.

Approaching the pet store that afternoon, she was surprised that she felt so calm. She opened the door and passed by the tropical fish and gerbils. Going right to Mr. Murphy's desk near the puppy cages, she said, "Mr. Murphy, I'm interested in the part-time job you advertised."

He cocked his head, frowning a little. "I've seen you here often, but you're rather young. I doubt that you could even get a work permit."

"I'm almost twelve," Laurie blurted out, suddenly feeling despair.

Mr. Murphy nodded. "Yes, too young. Tell me why you're interested."

Laurie explained her love for animals and that she might even want to be a vet some day. It also slipped out that she didn't care for baby-sitting.

Mr. Murphy grinned. "That gives me an idea. While I can't hire you, maybe some of my customers will. People often ask if we do dog walking. Other people, away for just a day, want someone to feed and pet a cat. I think I could recommend you for that service. What do you think?"

Laurie stood tall as a smile spread over her face. "Sure, Mr. Murphy. I can handle that. Will you help me decide what to charge?"

He nodded as he reached for a 3 x 5 card. "Why don't I call Mrs. Kratz for you right now? She left this card in case I heard of someone who'd walk her poodle."

Action Idea: God's answers to prayer often come in unexpected ways. Paul was surprised and delighted to receive the gift from the Philippians, easing his prison stay. Laurie didn't get the job she applied for but did get one more suited to her age and abilities. If you have a worry, pray about it particularly and with thanks for God's continuing blessings. Write down your prayer request. Write down other things in your life for which you're thankful to God. Be open to his answer. It may take awhile to come, but in the meantime he will ease your worry.

Bible Reading Extra: Philippians 4:6-7

Prayer: *Dear Jesus, you are my Savior, friend, and king. Forgive me for worrying, forgetting to trust you, forgetting to tell you my problems. Here's what's on my mind: _____ . You have always helped me in the past, and I thank you. Thank you for hearing me today. Keep my heart and mind open for your answer. Amen.*

4 Karen's Aunt Died

"Where, O death, is your victory? Where, O death, is your sting?"

1 Corinthians 15:55

St. Paul wrote two letters to the church in the great Greek city of Corinth. Some people were setting themselves up as new teachers there. They taught things that didn't agree with what Jesus said and taught. These people couldn't understand the resurrection of the body after death. They got many other people confused in the church at Corinth.

In his letter, Paul carefully explains the resurrection, comparing it to a seed which seems dead when put into the ground. But soon a new life comes out of that seed, new and beautiful and completely different. The life was put in there by God, the Creator.

Certainly our God who created all things can create new life even in death.

After explaining all this, Paul quotes an Old Testament passage which is our Scripture today. There is no sting in death. Death has no more power. Christ's victory through his death on the cross and resurrection gives us victory, too.

This is the assurance Paul wanted the Corinthian people to have. The words are there in the Bible for us, too.

Laurie had been walking Mrs. Kratz' white poodle, Boo-boo, on Tuesdays and Thursdays after school for about a month. The pet store manager also gave her jobs feeding cats on weekends and sometimes checking on canaries or parakeets. Sometimes the job kept her from doing things with her friends. When Karen's aunt died, Laurie wanted to do something to comfort her friend, but she was often busy.

"My aunt and I were so close," Karen explained on the phone one afternoon. "She took me to vacation Bible school in the summer, and I spent almost every other weekend at her house."

"I know," Laurie said sympathetically. Karen had been saying the same thing every time they talked for the two weeks since the aunt died. Laurie's mom had explained that grieving people need to talk about the death and the dead person, so Laurie listened. Sometimes she tried to say something about the aunt being with Jesus. Karen agreed but she still seemed miserable.

"Why don't you go dog walking with me today?" Laurie asked. Maybe doing something different with a friend would help, she thought.

"Well, I was going to write some thank-you notes for letters and flowers we received—" Karen began.

"You can do that tonight. Come on," Laurie urged. "It would be fun to have company. You'll like Boo-boo; he's a silly little dog."

Karen finally agreed, and Laurie explained to Mrs. Kratz that a friend would be working with her today. Then she and Boo-boo went to meet Karen.

"Look at that goofy dog," Karen said, laughing as Boo-boo barked at a mockingbird high in a tree. Then the poodle picked up a piece of scrap paper, shook it vigorously, dropped it and looked for a new adventure. A neighbor was planting tulip bulbs. Boo-boo grabbed one, shook it and spit it out.

"Hey!" said the man. "I won't have any flowers in the spring if you do that."

Laurie apologized and quickly pulled Boo-boo's leash. By the end of the dog walk, both girls realized they'd had a fun afternoon.

"Thanks for getting me out," Karen said. "I really needed something to do. I think you were an answer to my prayer about being lonely."

Laurie grinned. "I had fun too. Why don't we do it again Thursday?"

Action Idea: Friends who are grieving need words and deeds to help and comfort them. Everyone thinks, *I don't know what to do for my friend.* Often simply including the friend in an activity, as Laurie did, helps. The activity helps the person relax and the words about Jesus' love and the hope of resurrection seem surer. Is there someone, old or young, who needs your friendship because of grief? How could you include that person in some activity?

Bible Reading Extra: John 14:1-3

Prayer: *Lord Jesus, you have gone to prepare a place for us in Heaven. Sometimes it's hard to understand that. Although tulip bulbs seem dead when they are planted in the ground, new life sprouts from them. They grow into plants with beautiful flowers in the spring. We will be given new life after death, too, because nothing is impossible for you. Amen.*

1 Look at That Moon!

The heavens declare the glory of God; the skies proclaim the work of his hands.

Psalm 19:1

In this and the next verses of the psalm, the psalmist tells of God's glory seen in creation. From the time he was a young boy, looking after sheep on a hillside, David had watched the skies. As a poet, he saw much beauty there for his songs.

David's people were outdoor people. They worked outside. Their houses had flat roofs where they could sit and enjoy an evening breeze. The roofs were similar to the sundecks you see on some modern houses. Time was told by watching the moon and the stars. Not a day would pass when the skies wouldn't be watched for what they told about weather, time, and God's glory too. With no street lights and no tall buildings to block the view, people depended on "God's lights" day and night.

When David grew up and was having his troubles with Saul, David sometimes had to hide in caves. What comfort he found in the assurance of God's care as he looked at the sky! It reminded him that God's love and help were enough for him.

Violet awoke early in her city rowhouse. Peering out the window, she saw the early commuter bus roar by. The street lights gave enough light so Violet could pack her suitcase without waking her little brother. Then dad went over the bus directions once more. Violet was on her way to Aunt Ophelia's place in the country.

The street lights were off, and the morning haze from the traffic made Violet cough a little. At the corner she caught the X-12 bus out of the city, transferring at the edge of town to the Beach Express, taking her to the beach house Aunt Ophelia was renting for two weeks.

Violet couldn't believe her eyes and nose and ears when she got there. Walking with her aunt toward the sandy beach, something seemed to be expanding inside Violet.

"I feel like I could fly," she said. "I've never seen so much open space. The water's so blue-green and the sky's almost turquoise. My sky never looks like that."

"That's why I wanted you to come," Aunt Ophelia said as a seagull dove for a little fish. "You've never seen anything except the polluted city sky. The smog over the city blocks the view. Wait till you see the moon rise over the water and the sun come up in the morning."

That evening, Violet sat transfixed, watching the huge orange moon push above the horizon. Its light made a path across the water straight to where Violet sat. Bright stars dotted the blue-black sky. Slowly the moon turned golden, then bright silver-white.

"What do you think?" Aunt Ophelia asked, bringing Violet a cup of cocoa.

"I just see God loving us an awful lot. When I go home, I have to remember this is out here."

Action Idea: Vast, open spaces, the moon, stars, and sun do speak of God's glory and majesty. If you have a chance to really spend time looking at these today, think of David and his psalm. But if you are where you can't see the sky, consider something else in God's magnificent creation—a tree, a leaf, a moth. Write down a few thoughts about what this says to you about God. This same God loved us enough to send his son. How will your words about creation end with thoughts of Jesus?

Bible Reading Extra: Psalm 19:1-6

Prayer: *O God, how beautiful is your creation! And you made it for us. How deep is your love that you give in Jesus. Amen.*

2 Watch Your Little Brother, Please

Love is patient. Love is kind.

1 Corinthians 13:4a

You have probably heard or read this whole section on love from 1 Corinthians 13. It is well known and often quoted. But what kind of love is the Apostle Paul talking about?

He was writing to the church at Corinth. Some people there thought they had more knowledge than others. They thought they really knew it all. Paul said they were puffed up with pride. We might say they were stuck up. But knowledge that makes people stuck up doesn't come from God's Holy Spirit, Paul told them. True knowledge of God and his ways goes along with love—love for God and love for others in the church.

Paul told the people in Corinth: "Love is patient, love is kind. It does not envy, it does not boast, it is not proud. It is not rude, it is not self-seeking, it is not easily angered, it keeps no record of wrongs. Love does not delight in evil but rejoices with the truth. It always protects, always trusts, always hopes, always perseveres (1 Corinthians 13:4-7). This is the love that Christians are to have for each other, Paul says. It is a gift of the Holy Spirit. It is something to pray for.

Because our families can be a little part of the whole church, we can pray for this kind of love at home, too.

When Violet returned to the city after visiting her aunt in the country, she missed the beautiful night sky with stars and moon. But now she appreciated the trees that grew in little squares of dirt in the city sidewalk. One fall morning she roller skated down the sidewalk, noticing how the leaves were turning yellow and orange. *Pretty*, she thought.

Just then her father called. "Violet, I want you to watch little James while I'm gone this morning."

Ugh, thought Violet, turning to see her four-year-old brother James struggling toward her on his little roller skates. "Can't he just watch TV?" called Violet. "He always falls and throws a tantrum."

62

Father shrugged. "He has to learn sometime." He disappeared before Violet could protest again.

"Pull me fast, Vi," said James. But when they'd gone half a block, James changed his mind. "I can do it myself." He snatched his hand away and wobbled down the sidewalk on his own.

"Watch where you're going!" yelled Violet. "Watch the cracks." But she knew he wouldn't. He always wanted to watch his feet. "Look out!" she yelled, skating after him, but he tripped right into one of the dirt squares where a tree grew.

"OW!" James screamed.

Violet picked him up. He thrashed and kicked. "Well, just lie there then. You didn't hit the tree. You just scared yourself."

"I don't wanna skate." He yanked off a skate along with his sneaker, throwing them both down the sidewalk.

Violet took a deep breath. She remembered the little sign Mother had over the kitchen counter: "Love is patient and kind." *Well, God,* she thought, *I don't have it, but I sure need it. Please help me.*

As she retrieved the shoe and skate she saw a picture in her mind of herself when she was little and learning to skate. "Of course," she said aloud. She started talking gently to James. "That was a rough fall, James. But you wanna know how I learned to skate when I was little?"

He blinked and nodded, letting her put his shoe and skate on again.

"Around the corner, by Jones' store. You know the railing by the little parking lot? I used to hold it with one hand and skate back and forth. Want to try?"

James sniffed and nodded. Violet thanked God for getting her through the first crisis of her baby-sitting morning.

Action Idea: Often the little, everyday exasperations in family life require more love than a big crisis. How do you get along with others in your family? Is there one person with whom it's especially hard to get along? Ask God to give you love that is patient and kind. Then keep your imagination open for something new to come along.

Bible Reading Extra: 2 Corinthians 1:3-4

Prayer: *Dear Jesus, you have helped me before to love others in my family. Forgive me for forgetting to ask for help each time I need it. Please give me your love for _____ today. Amen.*

3 Just Leave Me Alone!

Very early in the morning, while it was still dark, Jesus got up, left the house and went off to a solitary place, where he prayed.

Mark 1:35b

Jesus had been teaching in the synagogue one Sabbath. People were amazed when they heard him. When he came out, he met a man with an evil spirit. Jesus healed the man, and the people were even more amazed. They crowded around. But Jesus left with some of his disciples for Simon Peter's house.

And here was someone else to heal—Peter's mother-in-law. Once she was well, she was able to

fix a meal for them. But soon the whole town gathered in front of the house. What a crowd! Jesus had had a long busy day, healing all sorts of diseases and driving out demons. He was God's Son but also a man, and he was weary after such a day.

He slept that evening but got up very early in the morning, before the crowds would be back again. Quietly, he slipped out of the house and found a place where he could be alone. He sighed and began to pray, having conversation with his heavenly Father.

It was good that he found that time alone, because soon Peter and his friends came looking for him. "Everyone is looking for you," they told Jesus. But Jesus knew they had to go on to the next town. He had much preaching and teaching and healing to do. And as he went on his mission, the crowds would get larger and larger. Again and again Jesus would have to take time and find a place to be alone with just his heavenly Father.

On the day Violet taught her little brother James to skate, he wanted Violet to do everything with him. "Read *my* book," he said, crawling up in her lap when she was trying to read her own book.

"James, I've played with you all day. It's my turn to read my book," she said, pushing him away. "Go help mother set the table or watch out the window for dad," she said, not even looking up.

James plopped down right on her feet and started "reading" his book aloud. Violet tried to ignore him.

"Vi," called mother, "will you make these calls for me?" She appeared with a list of PTA volunteers. "Remind them of the meeting tomorrow."

"Oh, mother, I'll do it later, OK?"

"Violet," mother said sternly, "please do it now. This is a good time to find people home."

"Violet won't read to me," James tattled, pulling on Violet's book.

It was too much. "Just leave me alone, everybody!" she cried, as she ran upstairs to her room. She slammed the door and fell across the bed. "No one understands," she sobbed. "I'm not Supergirl." Outside horns honked in the rush hour traffic. Violet cringed. Usually she didn't even hear the traffic, but now, in her need to be alone, everything pressed in on her. She wished she were at Aunt Ophelia's on the quiet beach, watching the moon. She remembered the peacefulness of being alone there. As she lay staring at the ceiling, her thoughts drifted and she looked around the room. The cross on the wall, her old stuffed bear, a picture of Jesus with the children and another of him praying alone. She closed her eyes, not knowing what to pray, just being alone with Jesus.

A loud crash and cry from downstairs shook her. James was obviously not helping mother in the kitchen. Violet felt a sudden need to pray for her mother. *I guess I can go down now,* she thought after a few minutes. *I think I can manage to help.*

Action Idea: If Jesus needed time alone with his heavenly Father, we need time alone, too, especially time to pray. Violet really needed some time alone. But what could she have done differently? Maybe if she'd said "OK" to her mother, but explained that she needed time by herself after dinner, she could have waited until later to be alone. If we give ourselves enough alone times, we're not so apt to blow up as Violet did. Consider your days. Plan some time to be alone with God each day for the next week. When you're with God, pray for all those with whom you live.

Bible Reading Extra: 1 Timothy 2:1-6

Prayer: *Dear Jesus, it's good to know about your alone times. Help me to plan special times alone with you so I can be loving in the together times with my family and friends. Amen.*

1 My Best Friend Changed

Some friendships do not last, but some friends are more loyal than brothers.

Proverbs 18:24 TEV

Here is another one of the wise sayings in the book of Proverbs. There are many reasons why friendships do not last. Sometimes friendship is only pretended. Then, when the pretender doesn't get his or her way, the friendship disappears. Other times people change and have different ideas about things. Rather than argue all the time, it can be better if the two go separate ways.

This happened to the apostles Paul and Barnabas. The two traveled together, spreading the gospel. But when Barnabas wanted to take Mark on one of the journeys, Paul was against the idea. The Bible tells us that they quarreled. Then each went his own way. This must have been a painful separation for two men who loved the Lord Jesus very much. But both are regarded very highly by the church. The Lord continued to use both men for his kingdom, although not working together.

Perhaps it was better that each went his own way rather than to keep arguing on and on. They could trust in the forgiveness of their sins, knowing God would be with them wherever each would travel.

"Hi, Jen!" Sally shouted, racing across the yard as soon as she saw the blue car pull up next door. Her best friend, Jennifer, was home after a summer at music camp.

Jennifer's long blond hair, in a single braid, fell across her shoulder as she got out of the car. "Hi, Sal. Here, take my stuff, will you? I'll get my violin."

Sally grabbed a green duffle bag and followed Jen and her dad into the house. Around the kitchen table, the girls caught up on the news. "You want to come over for supper?" Sally asked. "It's beef stew. Only two of mom's charges will be there." She referred to the day-care kids her mother watched. Sally had helped all summer with the kids' games and crafts. She was eager to show Jennifer some of the activities.

"Not tonight," Jen said. "We've been visiting

relatives for a couple of days coming back from camp. I really need to practice."

"Oh." Sally couldn't think of anything else to say, she was so surprised. She and Jennifer had always "lived" at each other's houses. And they still had so much catching up to do from summer. "Well, I guess I better go home and see if mom needs help."

During the next days, Sally realized more and more that things were different. When her mom came to say goodnight one evening, Sally told her what she'd been feeling. "It's not the same with Jen; the worst part is, I don't think it ever will be again. It's like we're just acquaintances, not best friends. She's so into her music now. I know she wants to be a musician, but oh, I don't know." Sally stared out the window into the dark night.

"Sometimes people change a lot. Jen probably thinks you've changed, too," mom said.

"Me? I didn't go to some special camp," Sally protested.

"No, but you really helped me with the children. And you know how you've said maybe you'd like to be a teacher or children's librarian or even an occupational therapist for children. You've developed special interests that take your time and so has Jennifer. Maybe one of your other friends needs you more."

Sally nodded. "Maybe so," she said, but right then she still felt sad.

Action Idea: Friendships do change. Sometimes it's very painful for the emotions. But our Lord Christ understands. He is the one friend who will never change; he will always be there for you. If you and a friend have changed so much that you're not close any more, perhaps it's time to stop fretting. Other friends may need your caring now more than the old friend. Plan to do something with one of these friends this week.

Bible Reading Extra: Acts 15:35-41

Prayer: *Lord, it hurts when people change and friendships become different. I don't know what to do then. Be with me. Help me to listen to you. Help me to give and accept friendship. And thank you for always being my best friend. Amen.*

2 Gossip—Right or Wrong?

Tell them not to speak evil of anyone, but to be peaceful and friendly, and always to show a gentle attitude toward everyone.

Titus 3:2 TEV

Paul wrote to Titus who was the leader of a new Christian church on the island of Crete. Titus really had his hands full with all sorts of problems. His Christians lived in a non-Christian community. People would laugh at the Christians and make fun of them.

Worse, in the church, some people thought they knew it all. These people thought of themselves as new leaders. They taught ideas that didn't agree with the gospel of Christ. The ordinary Christian became confused and didn't know whom to believe.

So Paul wrote to Titus, telling him how to encourage his Christians and how to keep harmony in the church. With so many conflicting ideas around, there was plenty of opportunity for discussion. Paul reminded Titus and the believers to be kind and gentle, to show by their actions that they were the true Christians. "Don't say evil things about others," he said.

Surely the people had to ask God to help them to be loving and kind. As they remembered the loving-kindness of Jesus, they were reminded to be kind and gentle, too. Sometimes it was very tough. But those are times we need reminders.

Sally sat at the lunch table with the kids from last year's fifth grade, all except Jennifer who'd gone to orchestra practice this year.

"Jennifer's never around to do anything," Alice said. "Ever since she went to that snooty camp, she's too good for us."

Sally swallowed a gulp of milk, washing down her peanut butter and honey sandwich. "I know," she said. "She hasn't been to my house for dinner once since she got back."

"Really?" said one of the other girls who knew Sally and Jennifer used to be best friends. She shook her head. "Figures."

Sally stared into her empty brown bag. Why had she said that about dinner? Hadn't she decided that things were going to be different—that it wasn't anybody's fault?

Alice offered everyone some of her homemade

cookies. "A nerd. She's just turned into a nerd. I heard she's even—"

"No, Alice, she's . . . she's . . . " Sally caught her breath to keep from yelling. She had to say this calmly. She had to make them understand. "Jennifer has a gift in playing the violin. It would be wrong for her to goof off and skip practicing just to be with us."

Alice's eyebrows shot up. "You just said she hadn't been to dinner—"

"I know. I miss her. But someday we'll all be glad to hear her play. She isn't snooty; she's just busy." Sally bit into the cookie Alice had given her. "This is yummy. What's in it?"

Alice smiled proudly. "Carrots," she giggled. "It's sort of a carrot cake recipe made into cookies. I made 'em last night."

Suddenly, the mood at the table seemed a little happier. Sally looked with interest at Alice. "I didn't know you could bake so well," she said. "Would you share the recipe? These would make good snacks for mom's day-care kids. She's always looking for something healthy, not too sweet."

The bell rang and the girls started back to the classroom. "Why don't you come over tomorrow after school? We can bake some together. I'm really into cooking these days," Alice said.

"Sure," Sally agreed. "Sounds good."

Action Idea: The dictionary defines gossip as either chatty talk or rumors of a personal nature. Often there's a tightening in the conscience of a Christian when the rumors start. Even though at first Sally joined in the talk about Jennifer, she soon steered the conversation to something positive. Try it yourself. Next time you find yourself listening to unkind, negative talk or nasty rumors, think of something kind, gentle and positive to say. Practice makes it easier.

Bible Reading Extra: Titus 3:1-8

Prayer: *Lord Jesus, it's easy to say unkind things, especially when I've been hurt by someone or don't like someone. Help me to remember that you died for that person, too. Give me your kind of love for _____ today. Amen.*

3   It Doesn't Feel Like Christmas

. . . and she gave birth to her firstborn, a son. She wrapped him in cloths and placed him in a manger, because there was no room for them in the inn.

Luke 2:7

For so many years a Savior had been promised. Israel longed for this Messiah who would rescue them. He was to be the Son of David, coming in the line of the beloved King David. His name would be called Wonderful, Mighty Counselor, the King of kings.

How Mary must have wondered when the angel first came to her! She would have a baby who would be the promised Savior? She hurried to tell her cousin Elizabeth. Then Mary prepared carefully for this special birth. But when it was almost time for the baby to be born, she and Joseph learned they must take a trip.

Off they went to crowded Bethlehem with Mary ready to give birth at any time. They heard the words, "No room here. You can stay in the stable, I suppose."

Where was God? Mary must have wondered. Was she really about to give birth to the promised Savior? Would God really want the King of kings to be born in a dark, damp stable with a bunch of smelly animals?

The answer was yes. Then even the poor, lonely, and common people would know that the Savior was for them too. He shared their kind of life. The Mighty God was born in an ordinary stable. It didn't seem like a birthplace for a king, but it was. How thankful we can be for the first Christmas.

Sally found that she could make Alice's carrot cookies into Christmas cookies, if she just decorated them with a little icing. She squeezed green icing to make a Christmas tree on a cookie. "It doesn't seem like Christmas without dad," she said to her mother who was folding clothes nearby.

"Well, you'll be going to visit him the week after Christmas. You'll get to celebrate Christmas twice," mom said. Sally could tell that her mom was trying to be cheery. But the first Christmas since her parents' divorce was not going to be much fun.

"I wonder what Mary thought about staying in the stable instead of an inn," mom went on. "God acts for us in surprising ways."

Sally thought about what a stable would be like. Maybe like our dark, damp garage. Who could imagine having a baby there? And then making a bed for him with the piles of old newspapers being saved for the Cub Scout drive. No cows or donkeys but plenty of spiders and maybe a mouse now and then. And suddenly Jesus comes, like a bright light into that dreary place, like the flashlight Sally used to find things in the dark.

"Mom, can I make a Christmas play with the day-care kids? I just got this neat idea. We can make the garage a stable. The kids can see how amazing it was that Jesus was born in that kind of place."

Mom nodded. "Yes, that might work. Amelia lives in a tiny two-room house not much bigger than the garage. She'd like to see Jesus in our garage."

"And Billy could bring his dog that day," Sally said. "He'd like to know that Jesus and the animals got along." She finished the last cookie and reached for a pad to write down ideas. It was starting to feel like Christmas.

Action Idea: Sometimes it doesn't feel like Christmas because we aren't thinking about the Christmas story—Jesus' birth as our Savior. When Sally started thinking about that, she discovered ideas for sharing the good news of Jesus. Try reading about the birth of Jesus in the first chapters of Luke and Matthew. Read different translations of the Bible. Let your mind daydream about ways to share Jesus. Jot down some of your ideas; then carry out at least one of these.

Bible Reading Extra: Isaiah 12:4-6

Prayer: *Dear Jesus, you came in the most ordinary kind of way. I feel at home with you. Help me to help a friend to feel at home with you, too. Amen.*

4　Faith

Now faith is being sure of what we hope for and certain of what we do not see.

Hebrews 11:1

Chapter 11 of the book of Hebrews in the New Testament is a great chapter about faith and faithful people. This book is really a letter written to a group of people who were in danger of losing their faith. The author wanted the people to be sure of their salvation and heaven, the things hoped for but which cannot be seen.

After this definition of *faith,* the writer lists some examples of faithful people from the Old Testament who might be called *heroes of faith*. He talks about Noah who had faith enough to build an ark as God instructed, even when it wasn't raining or flooding.

He talks about Abraham who had faith that God could make him and his wife parents, even in old age. People must have laughed and said *"Impossible!"* But Abraham believed and lived in God's loving care.

People today have "faith" in things like computers and telephones. Many people do not know how the things work, but they trust these devices to work. How much more we can trust God, the one who created the minds that designed computers and telephones. Our faith in God is often made stronger by seeing the faith of others, people like Abraham and people we know today.

Sally was in her garage, surrounded by little children from her mother's day-care business. "This will be Baby Jesus," she said, putting a doll into Amelia's arms.

Little Amelia's eyes lit up. "Ohh," she cooed, holding the doll tenderly.

Billy motioned to his dog who would be part of the Christmas play. "Stay!" he said to the shaggy dog. "You sit there. Be a watchdog for Baby Jesus."

But as the rehearsal went on, the children became restless. Everyone wanted to play with Billy's dog. Sally got exasperated at times.

On the evening before the performance, Sally stayed up late, working on costumes. Her mother was helping.

"This turned out to be more work than I thought," Sally said. "I always thought Christmas was a time for fun. I guess there's a lot of work in grown-up things."

Her mother finished the last pair of angel wings. "You can see how parents and teachers sometimes get so busy they forget about the real meaning of Christmas."

"Yes," said Sally, "and I started this play to help tell about Jesus for the children and their parents. Now it seems like a big hassle."

The next afternoon, just as it was getting dark, everyone assembled for the play. Parents sat in folding chairs in the driveway. Sally's neighbor friend, Jennifer, played "Away in a Manger" on her violin. Then Sally opened her Bible. "The Birth of Jesus," she announced and started reading from the second chapter of Luke.

The children carefully acted out the words. *How much they believe,* Sally thought as she watched. She glanced at the parents who were quiet, watching and listening. A couple of cars had stopped by the curb while neighbors watched too. For a few moments a group of busy people stopped to have their faith in Jesus renewed by a group of little children. *It* is *working,* Sally thought, and all her effort and worries were forgotten as her faith increased too.

Action Idea: Talking about Jesus is one way to share faith, but often doing something active is important. That can mean work as Sally found out. But her work was rewarded for herself and for others. Think of a way to share your faith during the Christmas or Easter season. Write down what you want to do so you'll know the effort required. Pray about your idea. Then use your time and energy to carry out your project.

Bible Reading Extra: Mark 10:13-16

Prayer: *Dear Jesus, it's so easy to let my faith be just nice thoughts about you. But I want to share my faith with _____ . Help me as I plan to _____ . You carried through with your plan to save me so I could live with you in Heaven. Please give me the energy and love to share the good news with others. Amen.*

DEBORAH

1   Stuck in the Middle

"Happy are those who work for peace; God will call them his children!"

Matthew 5:9 TEV

Jesus had been teaching and preaching about the kingdom of God. He had healed many people. Then one day he sat down and talked to his disciples about what it means to be part of God's kingdom. We might say, what it means to be a Christian. Jesus told about the happiness of a Christian in what's called "The Sermon on the Mount."

He spoke of the happiness of people in different conditions. Other translations say "blessed" instead of "happy" in the verse above. We are told that blessed means God has acted or is acting or will act for a person's good. We see that God cares about the person working for peace. This peace might be between nations or at school or in a family. God wants goodwill between people, and is pleased with people who strive for this goodwill or peace.

Jesus said that these people will be happy because they are close to God. Sometimes their lives will be difficult. The people may seem to have many troubles because it can be hard to make peace. But still, Jesus said that these people will have a special happiness that comes right from God.

Deborah squirted the hose against her dad's blue Chevy, rinsing the section she'd just washed. As she grabbed the sponge out of the sudsy bucket for the next section, her older sister Sheryl walked by.

"The hose is still running. You're supposed to turn it off when you're not using it," Sheryl directed. "You're wasting water."

"I turned the nozzle, but it won't go off all the way," Deborah explained, giving the nozzle another twist to demonstrate the problem.

Sheryl jumped back, shielding the white uniform she wore for her part-time job. "Don't squirt me! Just turn it off at the spigot." She turned and hurried down the block on the way to work while Deborah resisted the urge to yell something after her.

"Miss Bossy," muttered Deborah, tossing down the hose and reaching for the sponge again. But it wasn't in the bucket. She looked to see if she left it on the trunk of the car.

"Douglas!" she screamed. "What *are* you doing?" Her little brother sat on the driveway, making wet designs on the concrete with the sponge. "Now the sponge will be full of grit and it'll scratch dad's car. Boy, are you going to get it!" She said the last part, even though she knew Douglas wouldn't "get it." He was too little to know better. He never got in trouble because Deborah was expected to keep him *out* of trouble. She wished dad could see Douglas now. Then dad would realize what a pain that brother was.

Douglas splashed the sponge in the bucket, getting his overalls wet. "Let me help," he said.

"You do the tires," Deborah explained, demonstrating. "Just the tires. Daddy will like that." She rummaged in the trunk for another sponge to use on the rest of the car.

It sure is hard to be stuck in the middle, she thought. *Bossy big sister, pesty little brother.* She remembered the poem her mother showed her once about middle children. The poet understood how much patience was needed. Soon after that her memory work in Sunday school was "Blessed are the peacemakers." She was glad God had helped her be a peacemaker on the car-washing day. There could have been a quarrel two times, but Deborah kept the peace. As she thought about this, she knew God was giving her his special peace inside herself.

Action Idea: If you're a middle child, you know how Deborah felt. Sometimes it helps to talk to adults who were middle children. Check with your parents, Sunday school teacher, or another adult friend who was a middle child. God may use their experiences to help you. In being a peacemaker, you'll want to praise God for his goodness and help. The Bible Reading Extra is a wonderful song of praise.

Bible Reading Extra: Psalm 150

Prayer: *Dear Jesus, sometimes I'm bossed around. Sometimes I'm pestered. Be with me so I can be a peacemaker. Help me this week, especially with _____ . Amen.*

2   Everybody Does It

Do not conform any longer to the pattern of this world, but be transformed by the renewing of your mind.   .

Romans 12:2

In his letter to the Christians at Rome, the apostle Paul carefully explained why Jesus had come, lived and died for people. He told about the wonderful forgiveness people have because of Jesus. He was very clear about how much God loves people.

Then Paul told about the reaction people have to this wonderful love. People's lives will be different because people have felt God's love. They will want to please him. Paul says that the way of worship will

91

be different, too. People who have known God's love coming to them in Jesus will want everything they do to be a kind of worship.

That's when Paul gets to the verse above. If your life is to show God's love to others, you don't want to be like people who don't know God, copying everything they do. No, says Paul, let God change you from the inside out.

He means that if you stick close to God, listening to his Word, talking to him in prayer, God will help you be the kind of person he has made you to be. It won't be like obeying a set of rules. You will be God's kind of person by his power as you stay close to him. Paul knew this happened in his own life. He wanted other Christians to understand this wonderful new life with Jesus.

"Deborah, you aren't going to wear those jeans to school again," mom said. It was half a question and half a command.

"What's wrong with them? Sheryl has some just like them." Deborah retorted, knowing that sometimes she could use her older sister as an excuse.

"They're almost threadbare in the seat; that's what's wrong," mom said, "And Sheryl only wears her old jeans around the house."

Deborah fixed her shirttail to cover the seat of her jeans. "That's because in high school, everybody wears designer jeans. Sixth grade decided to be different this year. We're wearing old ones."

Mom rummaged in Deborah's closet and tossed out another pair of jeans. "These are old but not awful. I know you want to look like your friends, but sometimes you need to use your own good sense that God gave you. You wouldn't have pulled down your shirttail if you really thought those jeans were OK for school," mom said, sitting on Deborah's bed.

Deborah knew mom wouldn't leave until the jeans were changed. In silence Deborah put on the other pants. Mom smiled and nodded and left the room. Deborah looked at herself in the mirror. She really liked these jeans better. She looked more—more put together. She remembered what she'd thought the first time Sara Jane wore her awful jeans. *Gross! Who'd wear those to school!* But one by one, other girls in the class started wearing their worst jeans. Pretty soon anyone who wore half-way decent jeans felt weird. Then it seemed natural for Deborah to get out the old jeans she used for washing the car or mowing the lawn.

Maybe I'll start a new trend, Deborah thought. *I'll wear a nicer blouse too.*

Deborah entered the schoolroom feeling a little nervous but good about herself. "Oh, what a pretty blouse!" said Carrie.

"You going somewhere special after school?" asked Melanie.

"Thanks. No, I just felt like dressing up a little today," Deborah said. She had a feeling that tomorrow some of the other girls might be dressing up a little too.

Action Idea: Everyone is sometimes a leader, sometimes a follower. As a Christian, sometimes we decide not to be a follower as Deborah did. She became a leader in a better way, using the good sense God gave her, as her mother put it. Think of your life with other people. Are there things that you're doing that make you uneasy as God's child? Make a plan for doing something differently. Check the Bible Reading Extra. It will help you understand your parents' concern for you.

Bible Reading Extra: Psalm 78:1-8

Prayer: *Dear Jesus, I keep doing _____ . This is just like everybody else. You know it's hard to be different. You were different from others when you were on earth. But then you died and rose to forgive my sins. How I thank you! Please keep me near you. Amen.*

3   That's a Lie!

"You shall not give false testimony against your neighbor."

                                        Exodus 20:16

The above scripture verse is one of the Ten Commandments of God. You will remember that God gave Moses the Commandments after God rescued the people from being slaves in Egypt. God was leading them back to the promised land, the land he had promised to Abraham and his descendants.

The Commandments were part of an agreement with God. Because the people were grateful for being rescued from slavery, they were to obey God's commandments. The Commandments were also to make life more pleasant for people. But sin leads people to break the Commandments.

One of the worst times of accusing someone falsely came when people lied about Jesus. Mark 14:56-
57 tells about the many people who told lies about
Jesus at his trial. It is likely that these people had
told lies before. Often people lie about someone else
to make themselves look better or to win favor with
someone in authority. Or they may lie to keep themselves from getting into trouble, blaming their actions
on someone else. But God wants us to respect and
care about each other.

"Deborah!" Dad's voice sounded stern as he
called from the garage. She dropped the knives
and forks on the kitchen counter and went to see
what was the problem.

"Look." Dad knelt beside the front left tire of
his car. Little brother Douglas squatted down
next to dad. "The valve caps are gone. I was putting air in the tires today and noticed it. Doug
says you probably did it when you washed the
car."

"What? Dad, I wouldn't take off those little
things." She glared at smiling Douglas.

The four-year-old jumped up and ran to Deborah's bike. "For your bike tires. See!"

Deborah stared at the different valve caps on
her bike. "Dad, those aren't mine. I had silver
ones with little points."

Dad unscrewed the small black caps that were
now on Deborah's bike. "Well, *these* are mine all
right. Now I'd like to know where the other two

are." He looked at her as if she could produce the caps from thin air.

"Dad, I didn't take those. I don't know how they got on my bike. Douglas is fibbing again." She remembered the day she washed the car. "I let *him* wash your tires when I washed the car because he wanted to help."

Dad's voice was sharper. "Oh, come now, Deb. He can't screw and unscrew little things like this."

"I can't do it," Douglas echoed the words, shaking his head.

"Look, I don't know what's going on, Deb, but I think you'd better ride your bike down to the service station and buy more caps for the car."

Deborah could see it was useless to argue. Douglas scooted toward the house in front of dad. Deborah got her wallet and headed for the service station, wondering how she was going to finally prove she was innocent.

Mom discovered the evidence two days later on wash day. She held out the two black and two silver valve caps found in Douglas's pocket.

Action Idea: When Douglas realized his dad was upset about the missing valve caps, he protected himself by blaming the incident on his sister. What could he have done that would have kept harmony in the family? Have you ever been like Douglas? Or have you gotten in trouble because of false accusations as Deborah did? False accusations are very hurtful; Deb might never have been shown innocent.

This would affect how her parents treated her. If you have accused anyone falsely, ask God for help in setting things straight. He *will* help.

Bible Reading Extra: Isaiah 26:3-4

Prayer: *Dear Jesus, terrible lies were said about you. Help me to remember what lies about someone can do. Help me to protect other people's reputations by not saying untrue things about them. Amen.*

1   New School

". . . 'He is going ahead of you into Galilee. There you will see him just as he told you.' "

Mark 16:7

When Jesus was with his disciples, he told them several times he would have to die. But they couldn't grasp it. He was healing people, teaching with authority, doing amazing things. This dying didn't make sense.

At the Passover meal he spoke about a new covenant, a new promise, as he served the bread and wine. So much was going on. There was so much to think about with this wonderful man. How could he die? The disciples brushed aside the thought. They didn't understand at all when he said, "But after I have risen, I will go ahead of you into Galilee." (Mark

14:28). Peter was too busy talking about how he'd stick with Jesus no matter what. He didn't listen to these words about dying and rising to life.

And then it all happened—everything Jesus had talked about. Jesus was tried as a criminal; Peter said he never knew Jesus; Jesus was crucified and buried. What despair! It was all over. How terrible Jesus' friends felt.

The women went to the tomb to anoint Jesus' body with herbs, the custom of the times. The first surprise came when they saw the stone rolled away. But who was this young man in a white robe? He spoke kindly about Jesus and finished by saying that Jesus had gone ahead to Galilee, "just as he told you."

The women must have wondered, "Did Jesus say that?" Soon they would realize that he had and he was indeed alive. New joy and confidence in Jesus would be theirs. Later he would assure them that he would be with them always (Matthew 28:20).

"I don't see why we had to move," Cathy said to her father on a bright September morning. "We could have at least waited until I got out of sixth grade."

"At least we didn't move in the middle of the year," dad said. "I can remember moving in the middle of fifth grade when I was young."

Cathy grimaced. She was in no mood to hear about her father's school years. She looked out of the window of the car, seeing what other kids were carrying to school. Sack lunches. OK, she had one with her name on it. But backpacks? No-body had backpacks at home. They'd have felt weird on the school bus. Here she'd have to walk to school unless she could convince her parents to drive her often. She gripped her blue folder and checked that there was a pen and pencil clipped to the pocket inside.

"You're not coming in with me, are you?" Cathy asked.

"Not unless you want me to," dad said, pulling into a parking spot.

Cathy swallowed, wishing she were in first grade so she could say *yes*. But a sixth grader, walking in with her father. "No, I can find the office okay. It'll be marked," Cathy said trying to assure herself too.

Dad nodded. "I'll pray your day goes well, hon-ey."

Cathy walked briskly toward the red brick building. Around her kids were laughing and car-rying on like they'd known each other for years. In the office she stood in a line with other new kids, some with mothers, some with fathers. A tiny blond girl grinned at Cathy, showing missing teeth.

"I'm gonna be in first grade." She pulled on a chain around her neck. "See my new cross. I got a Snoopy lunch box too." She held up a blue Snoo-py box.

"Nice," said Cathy. "I like your cross." She bent down to show the girl the cross she always wore.

"I've got one, too. See." *Jesus is with us both,* she thought. *And dad is praying for me.* Somehow she wasn't so alone.

Action Idea: Cathy's cross reminded her that Jesus is with us always. Whenever we go somewhere, he's there first. Is there somewhere you'll be going for the first time soon? Pray about it. Ask someone to pray for you that day. Sometimes wearing a cross or other religious jewelry can remind you that Jesus is with you. Try it!

Bible Reading Extra: Genesis 12:1-7

Prayer: *Dear Jesus, help me to remember your name* Emmanuel *because it means "God with us." When I go to* _____ *remind me that you are there, just like you reminded your disciples. I thank you for your constant love and presence. Amen.*

2 I Think I'm in Love

He sets the time for love . . .

Ecclesiastes 3:8 TEV

Ecclesiastes comes right after the book of Proverbs, those tried and true sayings about living. Ecclesiastes seems to say that even if you follow all the rules for right living in Proverbs, life still has ups and downs. The book looks at life "under the sun" (that is, here on earth) and sees good times and bad times. Reading the book encourages us to see more than life "under the sun." We need to have God in the picture too. Then we can be sure everything is okay, no matter how it seems.

Because Jesus came to live on earth "under the sun" we can know he understands all our problems and our joys. One of these joys is a time for love.

There is a special kind of love that can grow between a boy and a girl, a man and a woman. By God's plan such love leads to marriage. Jesus blessed marriage by performing his first miracle at a wedding. His first miracle wasn't a healing but a simple giving of a gift to bless two people in love and their families. He gave wine when what was on hand ran out. He didn't want anything to spoil this day for two loving people who were probably friends of his.

But all love between boys and girls, men and women, does not lead to marriage. Because God has made us with emotions, you may begin to feel these emotions at your age. It is part of God's plan in making you ready for that special kind of love.

Cathy had been at the new school for a month. She had met a friend to walk to school with. She even bought a backpack so she could carry her books and lunch. But when Cathy stayed after school for volleyball on Tuesdays and Thursdays, she walked home alone. Her friend Barb didn't play.

For the last couple of days, Cathy was secretly glad that Barb wasn't there on volleyball days. Jimmy Turner, who stayed for flag football, walked Cathy's way. In class Jimmy sat by the windows. From her seat near the door, Cathy would note his wavy black hair and the cute way he'd put a finger up to scratch his ear lobe when reading something on the board. His voice was clear and steady when he answered questions.

When she answered, Cathy would see Jimmy staring at her, sometimes slightly nodding in agreement. If she glanced up, he'd grin and she couldn't help grinning back. There seemed to be some unspoken message between them.

Then, last Thursday, Jimmy had caught up with Cathy as she walked home after volleyball. "You can really serve," he said.

Cathy felt herself blush. "Thanks, that's the part I like best."

"You ever play tennis?" Jimmy asked, turning his head to look at her as they walked.

"No, I lived in the country before. There were no courts."

"You'd be a natural. Wanna play some afternoon? Or maybe after supper. It's still light for a while. We could walk back to school. I'll bring my sister's old racket for you, okay?"

Cathy nodded and tried not to sound as excited as she felt. "OK. I live in the white house at the end of this block. Wanna stop by around 6:30?"

That night Cathy lay in bed staring at the ceiling, smiling to herself. There was something awfully nice about spending time with Jimmy. She'd pick up the tennis swings fast, like he'd said. They planned to play on Saturday, too. "I wonder if this is love?" she said half aloud. She sighed, turned over and fell asleep.

Action Idea: Growing up is a learning time about many things including love. Today there are helpful books about understanding your feelings for boys, feelings that may be changing and new. Ask a parent, a Sunday school teacher, or someone in a Christian bookstore about such a book for your age group.

Bible Reading Extra: John 2:1-2, 11

Prayer: *Dear Jesus, thanks for going to that wedding. Thanks for loving your friends enough to give them wine out of water. Be with me as I get to know boys. Help me to be able to talk about you with them, too. Amen.*

3 Mom's Diary

*But Mary treasured up àll these things and pon-
dered them in her heart.*

Luke 2:19

In Old Testament times young girls married in their
teens. Mary was probably a teenager when the angel
told her that she would have a special child—the Son
of God. How amazed she was! But she must have
wondered when the baby was born in a stable!

Then excited shepherds arrived, telling of angels
and a glorious message. The scripture verse above
tells how Mary kept thinking about all that happened.

Later Mary and Joseph took the baby Jesus to the
Temple. An old man and a woman both recognized

the baby as the promised Savior and said so. Mary had more to think about.

The days and years went on. We know about the coming of the Wise Men, about Mary and Joseph's hurried trip to Egypt to keep the baby Jesus safe. But we know little about the years after that until the time when Jesus was 12. His parents had taken him to Jerusalem. On the return trip, he was missing. They looked for Jesus and found him teaching the teachers in the Temple. How extraordinary! Mary continued to store up memories, as if in a diary. Each of the events that Luke tells us about gave Mary another clue about the importance of her Son, Jesus. They do the same for us, too.

On a rainy afternoon, Cathy sat playing video games. "What'd you do when you were my age, mom? What'd you do when there weren't video games?"

Mom was writing a letter at her desk. "Watched TV or read, I guess," she said. "I forget. But look." She pulled a small green book out of a desk drawer. "I found my old diary when we moved. It's from fifth and sixth grades."

"Neat," said Cathy, turning off the set and reaching for the book. "Wow, and you tell me *I* have bad handwriting," she teased as she glanced at the scrawled pages.

Mom blushed. "It *was* pretty bad, wasn't it?"

Cathy curled her feet under her in a big chair.

While the rain splashed against the window, she got to know her mother as a young girl.

"Butchie ran away today. He was such a good dog and I know he doesn't like it here. Why did we have to move? I wish I could run away, too."

Cathy couldn't wait to find out what happened. "Did Butchie come back?" she asked.

Mom looked sad. "We found him two streets over. He'd been hit by a car. He was alive but died the next day."

"Oh, I'm sorry. You never told me that." Cathy felt her eyes water.

"Life is full of ups and downs. You'll find some good things there too," mom said.

Cathy read on.

"A new boy came to the beach this summer. Ronny Killdoo. I never thought freckles were cute before. He's so nice. Today we swam and went out in his canoe. In the evening he came to the cookout with all the beach gang. I hope we can do things all summer."

"What happened to Ronnie Killdoo?" Cathy asked.

Mom frowned, looking puzzled. Then she grinned. "He moved the next summer. Goodness, I forgot he was in there. Maybe you shouldn't find out all about me."

"Oh, but it's just like today. I mean you were sort of like me once."

Cathy hugged her mother. She was mom now

110

but once she was Margaret in Glenwood Elementary. It was good to know her both ways.

Action Idea: Other people's memories can be a blessing to us. Mary's memories give us wonderful details of Jesus' birth. Cathy's mom's memories, captured in a diary, helped Cathy feel closer to her mother. Why don't you share this devotion with your mother or a favorite aunt? Ask her about times when she was young.

Bible Reading Extra: Psalm 103:1-5

Prayer: *Lord Jesus, forgive me when I just think about* now. *I forget your blessings in the past. Stir up my memory of all the wonderful ways you have been special for me. Bless my parents and help me to remember that they have memories a lot like mine. Amen.*